T0142724

RAIDING THE CLOSET WITH SKELETON KEYS

Timika Latrice

Order this book online at www.trafford.com
or email orders@trafford.com

Most Trafford titles are also available at major online book retailers.

Printed in the United States of America.

ISBN: 978-1-4269-5506-8 (sc)

Trafford rev. 01/10/2011

 www.trafford.com

North America & international
toll-free: 1 888 232 4444 (USA & Canada)
phone: 250 383 6864 ♦ fax: 812 355 4082

Contents

Slide from the Ebony Tower

Please don't patronize me.
I can see you are being condescending.
I read between the lines well.
My brain can comprehend.
I wouldn't want to waste your energy
On word-searching conversations.

Please don't insult my intelligence.
I know what that last remark meant.
I have a vast vocabulary.
My small mind is larger than your dialect.
I see my new found strength upsets you.
I had to slide from the Ebony Tower
In order to feel the power of my own existence.

I see that once again your impulse is threatening.
You never could think,then react.
It's so pathetic to be sad,your reactive instinct.
So don't try to justify what you do.
Your moral compass malfunctioned a decade ago.

I still see my new found strength upsets you.
I am no longer blinded by your trickery.
I assume you want me to learn to come to terms with regards to you.
My friend,our bond was never that strong.
I learned early to detect a wrong.

I decided to slide from the Ebony Tower
To feel the power of my own existence.

I noticed you have an Ebony Tower of your own to slide down from.
Unless you enjoy basking in the Towers shadow.
In which case you will never feel the power of your own existence.

Once a month

Emotions on a bumpy rollercoaster ride.
Tears form in the blink of an eye.

My whole life rearranged once a month.
Sleeping patterns disturbed.
I become a pain-reliever junkie.
My body becomes tired.

I feel sick.
Everyone and everything seems louder.
Once a month's a bitch.

Sugar overdose

I'm on the verge of a sugar overdose.
Put more sugar on my cinnamon toast.
Sugar in my coffee.
Sugar in my tea.
Sugar made its way into my pee.

Give me lots of candy,
Cake with globs of frosting is what I crave.
I hope they bury me in a sugary grave.

Sugar cubes.
Sugar canes.
I injected melted sugar into my veins.
Sugar has a numbing effect on my brain.
Cups of sugar line my hallway.
I devour tons of sugar.

I'm on the verge of a sugar overdose.
Put some more sugar on my cinnamon toast.
Sugar in my coffee.
Sugar in my tea.
Sugar made its way into my pee.

Dracula got diabetes from drinking my blood.
Sugar my one true love.

Pure sugar cane runs through my veins.
I was buried in a sugary grave.

Tell me why

I have a voice that can barely be heard.
I have a soul that has an emptiness that can never be filled.
I have a heart as pure as new fallen snow,tell me why I can't be healed.

I have a mind that works like clockwork.
I have eyes that can make the strongest man crumble.
Tell me why I can't be healed.

I have a body that can run on empty.
I have legs that have walked the pathways of time.
Tell me why I can't be healed.

Black Widow

Warm arms embrace me.
Cool eyes comfort me.
Comfortable words glide from your tongue
Enchanting me.

A false sense of security comes over me.
Betrayal flows through your soul.
Letting coldness take control.

A web of deceit wraps around me.
Draining the light from me.
Spiders weave to no end.

Venom spews from your fangs.
Tearing down foundations.
Pitting one against another.
Never admitting a wrong.
Black widows stand alone.

Silent Scream

Arms like steel reach out to me.
The touch of his hand makes my skin crawl.

Eyes made of ice trace my figure.
The gaze he gives makes my blood boil.

His breath against my skin makes me shiver.
Like a newborn left uncovered in a still breeze.

He whispers words off the frailness of my soul.
He speaks of love while he holds me down against my will.
And tears my clothes as if they were pieces of unwanted paper.

He smiles a sick smile of hunger as he looks over my fully exposed body.
A silent scream welds in my body,as he opens my legs,
He pierces me with his manhood of steel.
He covers my mouth with his and invades me with his tongue.
Tears form in my eyes as I feel his manhood steal my innocence from me.
No-one can hear my silent scream.

The Cat Stole My Tongue

No words form in my throat.
I can't make a sound.
The cat stole my tongue.

I struggle to speak.
Nothing but nonsense makes its way from my lips.

My vocal cords are aching.
My heart is breaking.
Help me express myself.

No words form in my throat.
I can't make a sound.
The cat stole my tongue.

Makeway for the Motherload

Tick-tock of the clock.
Another day on the block.
Bang,bang someone call the cops.
Another persons shot.

Everyday it's the same thing.
Sounds of a ghetto spring.

Mom,call the kids,
They play where no-one is.

s-s-s-s-s goes my time bomb,
ready to explode!!

Makeway for the motherload!!

People aren't aware,
Nobody hears the fear in the hearts of our children.

Everyday it's the same thing sounds of a ghetto spring.

Urban Princess

Late at night,
The urban princess,
Is on the street,
Walking around with,
Platform shoes on her feet.

The red sequins dress,
She wears,twinkle like,
Rubies under the streetlights.

Nightclubs becomes her sanctuary,
Her problems disappear,cognac fills her voids.

She moves gracefully to the technosounds,
Her soul leaves her body,everyone stops and stares,no one touches her,
They wouldn't dare.

She walks out of the club without a care.The urban princess is on the
street with platform shoes on her feet.

Everybody has a darkside

Darkness lurks in the young and old.
Darkness wants to take control,making a playground of one's soul.

People are afraid to let the darkside be shown.
People are afraid of the unknown.

The darkside temps us all.
No mortal soul can resist the showcase evil of our fantasy world.
Lurking in the soul of every Holy man is a darkside.

Untouched Paradise

No sound filling my private space.
I'm tranquil as I sit thinking about my world.

When I open a window, no cars are rushing by with nowhere to go.
Just me in a world of rest going on my way.

When I walk down a street no man whistles my direction.
I am free to show my sexuality with no restrictions.

I dream about flying in the clear blue sky,while being naked and falling
free.

No sound fills my paradise.
No voice shall curl my blood.
My world will go untouched.

Hold me close

You gave me a thrill that I will never forget.
The way you touched me,you sent electricity flowing to my brain.

I never felt this way with a guy before,
Fill me with your love.
Hold my hand as we explore new places.

I want to feel you deep inside me.
Make me quiver with uncontrollable desire.

Ignite my fire with the flicker of your tongue.
Hold me as we make a new life.

Hold me close as we learn about love.
Move my body as we make love.
I need you near me,touch me.

Hold me close as I learn about love.
Move my body as we make love.

Naïve Princess

Once I was a naïve princess,
I looked at the world through rose-colored glasses.

Then one day,an older man came into my life.
He woke all my sleeping senses.
Said what I wanted to hear,soothed all my fears.

After a while,he began to pull away,
His interest in me started to fade.
I wouldn't hear from him for days,
His plans didn't include me,the avoidance was sickening.
He claimed to love me.

I was so naïve.

Once I was a naïve princess,
I looked at the world with rose-colored glasses.

Insomniacs

In my room wide awake.
Laying in bed.
Looking up at the ceiling.

I begin sorting my feelings.

Feelings of isolation and flustration.

I walk to the window.

I look down at the asphalt.
If I throw a glass through the window,
It wouldn't be my fault.

Feelings of anger,desire and insanity.

I'm in my room wide awake.
I better not stay up to late.

Coolest addiction

Brain waves are on overload.
Hearts are racing faster and faster.
What happens when you smoke the coolest addiction?

Sidewalk starts to boil.
Fish fall from the sky.
What happens when you smoke the coolest addiction?

Birds fly upside down and inside out.
The sun turns into a clown.
Blood comes from the growning weeds.
What happens when you smoke the coolest addiction?

People become monsters.
Water melts the skin.
Bugs crawl over the bed you sleep in.
What happens when you smoke the coolest addiction?

Body a rotting pile flesh.
Dirt covers your shallow grave.
This is what happens when you smoke the coolest addiction?

Chocolate Orgasms

Chocolate orgasms feel so good.
Actually better than they should.

Laying in bed in a bittersweet ecstasy.
Chocolate makes a slave out of me.

Chocolate tantalizes my tongue.
Me and Lady Godiva have so much fun.
I'm a whore who can't get enough.

Chocolate allows me to see why I enjoy being a woman.

Men should taste like cocoa or hot fudge syrup.
I would eat them up!

Chocolate orgasms rule the world!!

Learn about candy

Pathetic lies slide from your mouth,
Like a waterfall.
I see you standing in the light covering your face.
It's hard to keep a straight face,when you want to laugh like a hyena.

You use smiles to hide the truth.

Perhaps you think laughing will soften the truth.

I was there,it didn't.

I saw the truth cut right to the bone.
I wiped the bitter tears from the hurting eyes.

I hope we can find some sweet candy closure.
To heal the broken souls.

Fiennes bitter solitude

He walks into the home.
No one greets him in the evening.
No pictures hanging on the wall.

Solitude his only companion.
He sits in the dark listening to the suicide ballads on the radio.
Old memories plaque his mind.
Time appears to stand still.
The darkness his sanctuary.

The phone rings,but he can't answer.
The ring pierces the calm,rattling his nerves.
He yanks the phone out of the wall.
His beloved silence returns as a lovely mistress.

Solitude his sole companion.
The serenity coax his inner turmoil.
Caressing him to a delicate slumber.

Sheer anxiety

Anxiety makes me anxious.
Apologies make me apologetic.

I should soak my head in ice water.
I should try to be a better daughter.

I should set the world on fire.
I can be such a lair.

Anxiety makes me anxious.
Apologies make me apologetic.

Maybe I should call it a night,and turn out the light.
Or perhaps I should turn on a spotlight,then hide.

Anxiety makes me anxious.
Apologies make me apologetic.

Lizard Wine

Cold hand grasps the vodka bottle,
Swallow down the warm liquid,
Intoxicate your sleepy existence.

Vodka romance in a frosted crystal bottle,
Feeding your alcoholic lust.

Vodka your mistress in a beaded evening gown,
Let her seduce your fragile ego.

Under her intoxicating spell you forget how to be human,when she has
you in a sexy embrace.
She has you blinded by drunken kisses.

Your romance has devastating consequences.
You ended by being embalmed in Vodka.
The bar no longer has your chair reserved.

Wounded Pride

I crawl across the floor gathering shattered pieces of my wounded pride.
I collect the pieces desperately trying to make them fit.
I use glue to hold the pieces together.
I place my wounded pride back on the shelf.

Putrid potion

Look in my eyes,you will see a young woman searching for an identity.
I'm an intellectual prisoner in my own frame of mind.
I wake up to an endless void of despair.
I sit idle on the sidelines of life.

Escape comes to me in the form of creative expression.
I'm a lackadaisical tourist having a hard time relating fact from fiction.
Dementia slowly bleeds the sanity from my immortal soul.

I can't wake up from this nightmare

I can't wake up from this nightmare.
I can't hide my tears inside.
I can't wake up from this nightmare.
All those years I spent as your prisoner,
I had no choice,but surrender.

All those bruises I hide.
All those tears I cried.
The pain is killing my inside.
I can't wake up from this nightmare.

I don't know if I'll survive another year,in isolation and fear.
Every move I make is crucial.
The next move could be fatal.

I can't wake up from this nightmare.
I can't hide my pain inside.
Someone wake me up from this nightmare.

I only have this life to spare.

Sheer Ecstasy

I can feel your hand against my skin.
We are about to commit a sin,over and over again.

I can taste your skin.
I can see where my fingernails went.

I was blinded by sheer ecstasy.
I've never had that feeling come over me.

Your kisses send me spinning
Your touch leaves me trembling.
I'm calling out your name by the candle's flame.
I was blinded by sheer ecstasy,I've never had that feeling come over me.

Ooh,baby what you do to me,unlocks the desire deep inside.
I will never be the same.
I was blinded by sheer ecstasy.

Pay the Piper

I told you I think you are a disgrace.
Should've seen that pathetic look on your face.
Tears have the nerve to form in your cold eyes.
I don't understand why?
You are the one with the venomous lies.

No tears were formed when you ripped out my heart.
No mercy was shown when I was devastated by your betrayal.
You treated me like nothing.
I was just a conquest on your soul burning journey.

Now the time has come to pay the piper.
I want to bash you in the head I want to kick
You till you're dead.

I don't want to be your puppet anymore.
I won't let you treat me like a whore.
I finally have the strength to be free.
You no longer can manipulate me.

Now the time has come to pay the piper.
I want to bash you in the head I want to
Kick you till you're dead.

Tales of an alcoholic junkie

The smell of stale liquor on your breathe.
I can still taste it after we had sex.

I was slightly intoxicated by your drunken kisses.
Which sent me into ecstasy.
You always have that affect on me.

My eyes somehow have finally opened wide.
I can see the truth through your lies.

I always wondered what took me so long.
I probably felt sympathy for your pathetic childhood.
The maternal instinct came out in me.

You drank yourself blind and vomited all over the floor,I cleaned it up,while you stumbled to bed.

In the morning,you don't remember what was done or what was said, selective
Amnesia in your head.

Suicide watch

She confiscated all my razorblades.
She told me to try to survive for a day.
How the fuck did this turn out this way?

They got me in the Psych Ward,restrained to a bed,to get these damn suicidial thoughts out of my head.

I'm on a suicide watch.

I'm a medicated zombie,the devil himself wouldn't recognize me,he was the one who spawned me.

The psychiatrist told me to get a grip on reality.
So,I grabbed him around his fuckin' neck.
Are we having fun yet?

Jack ain't the only one over that cuckoo's nest.

I'm on a suicide watch.

I committed suicide,the damn neighborhood watched.

The perfect infliction(just no use)

A body lying on the wooden floor.
All that blood on the floor and all over the walls.
You run home trying to find an escape.
You go into the bathroom to splash cold water on your face.

It's just no use.
The image haunts you,the screams taunt you.

Your heart darkened,your soul belongs to Lucifer now.

All because she wouldn't love you.
You hate rejection of any kind.
You used a knife to end her life.

It's just no use.
The image haunts you,the screams taunt you.

You've gone insane,her ghost haunts you from the grave.
Confess your sins.

Homicidal Rage

Homicidal rage running through my brain.
Total destruction sparkles in my eyes.
I'm just a few steps from losing my mind.
So hard to keep this burning desire inside.
Homicidal rage injected warm into my ice veins.
Rage a fire in my cold heart.
Blood on my hands.
I show no pity to man
Homicidal rage surging through my brain.

99 years on Alcatraz

I am sentenced with no chance of parole.
The judge had no mercy on my soul.
I'm sent to a cell.a place not to far from hell.
In this prison no one can hear you yell.
99 years on Alcatraz.how long do you think I'll last?

I can feel my insides as they start to mold.
I can see myself growing old.
I feel like a lost soul.
99 years on Alcatraz,how long do you think I'll last?

The sun is shining through the bars.
The light reflects off my emotional scars.
At night time I don't see any stars.
I finally see things the way they are.
Somewhere along the line I got a beating heart.
99 years on Alcatraz,how long did you think I'd last?
My final question as they zipped up the body bag.
It seems that the justice system got the last laugh.
99 years on Alcatraz,you knew I wouldn't last!